ONE BIBLE VERSE A DAY

Name: _____

Start Date:

_____

Finish Date:

_____

| Bible Verse: _____ | Today's Date: _____ |

SAY, PRAY, & WRITE THE VERSE:

_____
_____
_____
_____
_____
_____
_____
_____
_____

| Bible Verse: _____ | Today's Date: _____ |

SAY, PRAY, & WRITE THE VERSE:

_____
_____
_____
_____
_____
_____
_____
_____
_____

| Bible Verse: _____ | Today's Date: _____ |

SAY, PRAY, & WRITE THE VERSE:

_____
_____
_____
_____
_____
_____
_____
_____
_____

Bible Verse: _____ **Today's Date:** _____

SAY, PRAY, & WRITE THE VERSE:

_____
_____
_____
_____
_____
_____
_____
_____
_____
_____

Bible Verse: _____ **Today's Date:** _____

SAY, PRAY, & WRITE THE VERSE:

_____
_____
_____
_____
_____
_____
_____
_____
_____
_____

Bible Verse: _____ **Today's Date:** _____

SAY, PRAY, & WRITE THE VERSE:

_____
_____
_____
_____
_____
_____
_____
_____
_____

Bible Verse: _____ **Today's Date:** _____

SAY, PRAY, & WRITE THE VERSE:

Bible Verse: _____ **Today's Date:** _____

SAY, PRAY, & WRITE THE VERSE:

Bible Verse: _____ **Today's Date:** _____

SAY, PRAY, & WRITE THE VERSE:

Bible Verse: _____ **Today's Date:** _____

SAY, PRAY, & WRITE THE VERSE:

Bible Verse: _____ **Today's Date:** _____

SAY, PRAY, & WRITE THE VERSE:

Bible Verse: _____ **Today's Date:** _____

SAY, PRAY, & WRITE THE VERSE:

Bible Verse: _____ **Today's Date:** _____

SAY, PRAY, & WRITE THE VERSE:

_____

_____

_____

_____

_____

_____

_____

_____

Bible Verse: _____ **Today's Date:** _____

SAY, PRAY, & WRITE THE VERSE:

_____

_____

_____

_____

_____

_____

_____

_____

Bible Verse: _____ **Today's Date:** _____

SAY, PRAY, & WRITE THE VERSE:

_____

_____

_____

_____

_____

_____

_____

_____

Bible Verse: _____ **Today's Date:** _____

SAY, PRAY, & WRITE THE VERSE:

_____
_____
_____
_____
_____
_____
_____
_____
_____
_____

Bible Verse: _____ **Today's Date:** _____

SAY, PRAY, & WRITE THE VERSE:

_____
_____
_____
_____
_____
_____
_____
_____
_____
_____

Bible Verse: _____ **Today's Date:** _____

SAY, PRAY, & WRITE THE VERSE:

_____
_____
_____
_____
_____
_____
_____
_____
_____
_____

Bible Verse: _____ Today's Date: _____

SAY, PRAY, & WRITE THE VERSE:

_____
_____
_____
_____
_____
_____
_____
_____
_____
_____

Bible Verse: _____ Today's Date: _____

SAY, PRAY, & WRITE THE VERSE:

_____
_____
_____
_____
_____
_____
_____
_____
_____
_____

Bible Verse: _____ Today's Date: _____

SAY, PRAY, & WRITE THE VERSE:

_____
_____
_____
_____
_____
_____
_____
_____

Bible Verse: _____ Today's Date: _____

SAY, PRAY, & WRITE THE VERSE:

Bible Verse: _____ Today's Date: _____

SAY, PRAY, & WRITE THE VERSE:

Bible Verse: _____ Today's Date: _____

SAY, PRAY, & WRITE THE VERSE:

10

Bible Verse: _____ Today's Date: _____

SAY, PRAY, & WRITE THE VERSE:

Bible Verse: _____ Today's Date: _____

SAY, PRAY, & WRITE THE VERSE:

Bible Verse: _____ Today's Date: _____

SAY, PRAY, & WRITE THE VERSE:

Bible Verse: _____ **Today's Date:** _____

SAY, PRAY, & WRITE THE VERSE:

Bible Verse: _____ **Today's Date:** _____

SAY, PRAY, & WRITE THE VERSE:

Bible Verse: _____ **Today's Date:** _____

SAY, PRAY, & WRITE THE VERSE:

Bible Verse: _____ **Today's Date:** _____

SAY, PRAY, & WRITE THE VERSE:
_____
_____
_____
_____
_____
_____
_____
_____
_____

Bible Verse: _____ **Today's Date:** _____

SAY, PRAY, & WRITE THE VERSE:
_____
_____
_____
_____
_____
_____
_____
_____
_____

Bible Verse: _____ **Today's Date:** _____

SAY, PRAY, & WRITE THE VERSE:
_____
_____
_____
_____
_____
_____
_____
_____
_____

Bible Verse: _____ **Today's Date:** _____

SAY, PRAY, & WRITE THE VERSE:

Bible Verse: _____ **Today's Date:** _____

SAY, PRAY, & WRITE THE VERSE:

Bible Verse: _____ **Today's Date:** _____

SAY, PRAY, & WRITE THE VERSE:

Bible Verse: _____ **Today's Date:** _____

SAY, PRAY, & WRITE THE VERSE:

Bible Verse: _____ **Today's Date:** _____

SAY, PRAY, & WRITE THE VERSE:

Bible Verse: _____ **Today's Date:** _____

SAY, PRAY, & WRITE THE VERSE:

Bible Verse: _____ **Today's Date:** _____

SAY, PRAY, & WRITE THE VERSE:

_____
_____
_____
_____
_____
_____
_____
_____
_____
_____

Bible Verse: _____ **Today's Date:** _____

SAY, PRAY, & WRITE THE VERSE:

_____
_____
_____
_____
_____
_____
_____
_____
_____
_____

Bible Verse: _____ **Today's Date:** _____

SAY, PRAY, & WRITE THE VERSE:

_____
_____
_____
_____
_____
_____
_____
_____
_____
_____

Bible Verse: _____ **Today's Date:** _____

SAY, PRAY, & WRITE THE VERSE:

_____
_____
_____
_____
_____
_____
_____

Bible Verse: _____ **Today's Date:** _____

SAY, PRAY, & WRITE THE VERSE:

_____
_____
_____
_____
_____
_____
_____

Bible Verse: _____ **Today's Date:** _____

SAY, PRAY, & WRITE THE VERSE:

_____
_____
_____
_____
_____
_____
_____

Bible Verse: _____ **Today's Date:** _____

SAY, PRAY, & WRITE THE VERSE:

_____
_____
_____
_____
_____
_____
_____
_____
_____

Bible Verse: _____ **Today's Date:** _____

SAY, PRAY, & WRITE THE VERSE:

_____
_____
_____
_____
_____
_____
_____
_____
_____

Bible Verse: _____ **Today's Date:** _____

SAY, PRAY, & WRITE THE VERSE:

_____
_____
_____
_____
_____
_____
_____
_____
_____

Bible Verse: _____ **Today's Date:** _____

SAY, PRAY, & WRITE THE VERSE:

_____
_____
_____
_____
_____
_____
_____
_____
_____

Bible Verse: _____ **Today's Date:** _____

SAY, PRAY, & WRITE THE VERSE:

_____
_____
_____
_____
_____
_____
_____
_____
_____

Bible Verse: _____ **Today's Date:** _____

SAY, PRAY, & WRITE THE VERSE:

_____
_____
_____
_____
_____
_____
_____
_____
_____

Bible Verse: _____ **Today's Date:** _____

SAY, PRAY, & WRITE THE VERSE:

_____
_____
_____
_____
_____
_____
_____
_____
_____

Bible Verse: _____ **Today's Date:** _____

SAY, PRAY, & WRITE THE VERSE:

_____
_____
_____
_____
_____
_____
_____
_____
_____

Bible Verse: _____ **Today's Date:** _____

SAY, PRAY, & WRITE THE VERSE:

_____
_____
_____
_____
_____
_____
_____
_____
_____

Bible Verse: _____ **Today's Date:** _____

SAY, PRAY, & WRITE THE VERSE:

_____
_____
_____
_____
_____
_____
_____
_____
_____

Bible Verse: _____ **Today's Date:** _____

SAY, PRAY, & WRITE THE VERSE:

_____
_____
_____
_____
_____
_____
_____
_____
_____

Bible Verse: _____ **Today's Date:** _____

SAY, PRAY, & WRITE THE VERSE:

_____
_____
_____
_____
_____
_____
_____
_____
_____

Bible Verse: _____ **Today's Date:** _____

SAY, PRAY, & WRITE THE VERSE:

_____
_____
_____
_____
_____
_____
_____
_____
_____

Bible Verse: _____ **Today's Date:** _____

SAY, PRAY, & WRITE THE VERSE:

_____
_____
_____
_____
_____
_____
_____
_____
_____

Bible Verse: _____ **Today's Date:** _____

SAY, PRAY, & WRITE THE VERSE:

_____
_____
_____
_____
_____
_____
_____
_____
_____

Bible Verse: _____ Today's Date: _____

SAY, PRAY, & WRITE THE VERSE:

_____
_____
_____
_____
_____
_____
_____
_____

Bible Verse: _____ Today's Date: _____

SAY, PRAY, & WRITE THE VERSE:

_____
_____
_____
_____
_____
_____
_____
_____

Bible Verse: _____ Today's Date: _____

SAY, PRAY, & WRITE THE VERSE:

_____
_____
_____
_____
_____
_____
_____

Bible Verse: _____ **Today's Date:** _____

SAY, PRAY, & WRITE THE VERSE:

_____
_____
_____
_____
_____
_____
_____
_____

Bible Verse: _____ **Today's Date:** _____

SAY, PRAY, & WRITE THE VERSE:

_____
_____
_____
_____
_____
_____
_____
_____

Bible Verse: _____ **Today's Date:** _____

SAY, PRAY, & WRITE THE VERSE:

_____
_____
_____
_____
_____
_____
_____
_____

Bible Verse: _____ **Today's Date:** _____

SAY, PRAY, & WRITE THE VERSE:

_____

_____

_____

_____

_____

_____

_____

_____

_____

Bible Verse: _____ **Today's Date:** _____

SAY, PRAY, & WRITE THE VERSE:

_____

_____

_____

_____

_____

_____

_____

_____

_____

Bible Verse: _____ **Today's Date:** _____

SAY, PRAY, & WRITE THE VERSE:

_____

_____

_____

_____

_____

_____

_____

_____

_____

Bible Verse: _____ **Today's Date:** _____

SAY, PRAY, & WRITE THE VERSE:

_____
_____
_____
_____
_____
_____
_____
_____
_____

Bible Verse: _____ **Today's Date:** _____

SAY, PRAY, & WRITE THE VERSE:

_____
_____
_____
_____
_____
_____
_____
_____
_____

Bible Verse: _____ **Today's Date:** _____

SAY, PRAY, & WRITE THE VERSE:

_____
_____
_____
_____
_____
_____
_____
_____
_____

Bible Verse: _____ Today's Date: _____

SAY, PRAY, & WRITE THE VERSE:

_____
_____
_____
_____
_____
_____
_____
_____
_____

Bible Verse: _____ Today's Date: _____

SAY, PRAY, & WRITE THE VERSE:

_____
_____
_____
_____
_____
_____
_____
_____
_____

Bible Verse: _____ Today's Date: _____

SAY, PRAY, & WRITE THE VERSE:

_____
_____
_____
_____
_____
_____
_____
_____
_____

Bible Verse: _____ **Today's Date:** _____

SAY, PRAY, & WRITE THE VERSE:

_____
_____
_____
_____
_____
_____
_____
_____
_____
_____

Bible Verse: _____ **Today's Date:** _____

SAY, PRAY, & WRITE THE VERSE:

_____
_____
_____
_____
_____
_____
_____
_____
_____
_____

Bible Verse: _____ **Today's Date:** _____

SAY, PRAY, & WRITE THE VERSE:

_____
_____
_____
_____
_____
_____
_____
_____
_____
_____

Bible Verse: _____ **Today's Date:** _____

SAY, PRAY, & WRITE THE VERSE:

_____
_____
_____
_____
_____
_____
_____
_____

Bible Verse: _____ **Today's Date:** _____

SAY, PRAY, & WRITE THE VERSE:

_____
_____
_____
_____
_____
_____
_____
_____

Bible Verse: _____ **Today's Date:** _____

SAY, PRAY, & WRITE THE VERSE:

_____
_____
_____
_____
_____
_____
_____
_____

Bible Verse: _____ **Today's Date:** _____

SAY, PRAY, & WRITE THE VERSE:

_____
_____
_____
_____
_____
_____
_____
_____
_____

Bible Verse: _____ **Today's Date:** _____

SAY, PRAY, & WRITE THE VERSE:

_____
_____
_____
_____
_____
_____
_____
_____

Bible Verse: _____ **Today's Date:** _____

SAY, PRAY, & WRITE THE VERSE:

_____
_____
_____
_____
_____
_____
_____
_____

Bible Verse: _____ **Today's Date:** _____

SAY, PRAY, & WRITE THE VERSE:

_____
_____
_____
_____
_____
_____
_____
_____
_____

Bible Verse: _____ **Today's Date:** _____

SAY, PRAY, & WRITE THE VERSE:

_____
_____
_____
_____
_____
_____
_____
_____
_____

Bible Verse: _____ **Today's Date:** _____

SAY, PRAY, & WRITE THE VERSE:

_____
_____
_____
_____
_____
_____
_____
_____
_____

Bible Verse: _____ **Today's Date:** _____

SAY, PRAY, & WRITE THE VERSE:

_____
_____
_____
_____
_____
_____
_____
_____
_____

Bible Verse: _____ **Today's Date:** _____

SAY, PRAY, & WRITE THE VERSE:

_____
_____
_____
_____
_____
_____
_____
_____
_____

Bible Verse: _____ **Today's Date:** _____

SAY, PRAY, & WRITE THE VERSE:

_____
_____
_____
_____
_____
_____
_____
_____

Bible Verse: _____ Today's Date: _____

SAY, PRAY, & WRITE THE VERSE:

_____
_____
_____
_____
_____
_____
_____
_____
_____

Bible Verse: _____ Today's Date: _____

SAY, PRAY, & WRITE THE VERSE:

_____
_____
_____
_____
_____
_____
_____
_____
_____

Bible Verse: _____ Today's Date: _____

SAY, PRAY, & WRITE THE VERSE:

_____
_____
_____
_____
_____
_____
_____
_____
_____

Bible Verse: _____ **Today's Date:** _____

SAY, PRAY, & WRITE THE VERSE:

_____
_____
_____
_____
_____
_____
_____
_____
_____

Bible Verse: _____ **Today's Date:** _____

SAY, PRAY, & WRITE THE VERSE:

_____
_____
_____
_____
_____
_____
_____
_____
_____

Bible Verse: _____ **Today's Date:** _____

SAY, PRAY, & WRITE THE VERSE:

_____
_____
_____
_____
_____
_____
_____
_____
_____

Bible Verse: _____ **Today's Date:** _____

SAY, PRAY, & WRITE THE VERSE:

Bible Verse: _____ **Today's Date:** _____

SAY, PRAY, & WRITE THE VERSE:

Bible Verse: _____ **Today's Date:** _____

SAY, PRAY, & WRITE THE VERSE:

Bible Verse: _____ **Today's Date:** _____

SAY, PRAY, & WRITE THE VERSE:

_____
_____
_____
_____
_____
_____
_____
_____
_____
_____

Bible Verse: _____ **Today's Date:** _____

SAY, PRAY, & WRITE THE VERSE:

_____
_____
_____
_____
_____
_____
_____
_____
_____
_____

Bible Verse: _____ **Today's Date:** _____

SAY, PRAY, & WRITE THE VERSE:

_____
_____
_____
_____
_____
_____
_____
_____

Bible Verse: _____ **Today's Date:** _____

SAY, PRAY, & WRITE THE VERSE:

_____

_____

_____

_____

_____

_____

_____

_____

Bible Verse: _____ **Today's Date:** _____

SAY, PRAY, & WRITE THE VERSE:

_____

_____

_____

_____

_____

_____

_____

_____

Bible Verse: _____ **Today's Date:** _____

SAY, PRAY, & WRITE THE VERSE:

_____

_____

_____

_____

_____

_____

_____

_____

Bible Verse: _____ **Today's Date:** _____

SAY, PRAY, & WRITE THE VERSE:

_____
_____
_____
_____
_____
_____
_____
_____
_____

Bible Verse: _____ **Today's Date:** _____

SAY, PRAY, & WRITE THE VERSE:

_____
_____
_____
_____
_____
_____
_____
_____
_____

Bible Verse: _____ **Today's Date:** _____

SAY, PRAY, & WRITE THE VERSE:

_____
_____
_____
_____
_____
_____
_____
_____
_____

Bible Verse: _____ **Today's Date:** _____

SAY, PRAY, & WRITE THE VERSE:

_____
_____
_____
_____
_____
_____
_____
_____
_____

Bible Verse: _____ **Today's Date:** _____

SAY, PRAY, & WRITE THE VERSE:

_____
_____
_____
_____
_____
_____
_____
_____
_____

Bible Verse: _____ **Today's Date:** _____

SAY, PRAY, & WRITE THE VERSE:

_____
_____
_____
_____
_____
_____
_____
_____
_____

Bible Verse: _____ **Today's Date:** _____

SAY, PRAY, & WRITE THE VERSE:

Bible Verse: _____ **Today's Date:** _____

SAY, PRAY, & WRITE THE VERSE:

Bible Verse: _____ **Today's Date:** _____

SAY, PRAY, & WRITE THE VERSE:

Bible Verse: _____ **Today's Date:** _____

SAY, PRAY, & WRITE THE VERSE:

_____
_____
_____
_____
_____
_____
_____
_____
_____

Bible Verse: _____ **Today's Date:** _____

SAY, PRAY, & WRITE THE VERSE:

_____
_____
_____
_____
_____
_____
_____
_____
_____

Bible Verse: _____ **Today's Date:** _____

SAY, PRAY, & WRITE THE VERSE:

_____
_____
_____
_____
_____
_____
_____
_____
_____

Bible Verse: _____ **Today's Date:** _____

SAY, PRAY, & WRITE THE VERSE:

_____
_____
_____
_____
_____
_____
_____
_____
_____

Bible Verse: _____ **Today's Date:** _____

SAY, PRAY, & WRITE THE VERSE:

_____
_____
_____
_____
_____
_____
_____
_____
_____

Bible Verse: _____ **Today's Date:** _____

SAY, PRAY, & WRITE THE VERSE:

_____
_____
_____
_____
_____
_____
_____
_____
_____

Bible Verse: _____ **Today's Date:** _____

SAY, PRAY, & WRITE THE VERSE:

_____

_____

_____

_____

_____

_____

_____

_____

Bible Verse: _____ **Today's Date:** _____

SAY, PRAY, & WRITE THE VERSE:

_____

_____

_____

_____

_____

_____

_____

_____

Bible Verse: _____ **Today's Date:** _____

SAY, PRAY, & WRITE THE VERSE:

_____

_____

_____

_____

_____

_____

_____

_____

Bible Verse: _____ **Today's Date:** _____

SAY, PRAY, & WRITE THE VERSE:

_____
_____
_____
_____
_____
_____
_____
_____
_____

Bible Verse: _____ **Today's Date:** _____

SAY, PRAY, & WRITE THE VERSE:

_____
_____
_____
_____
_____
_____
_____
_____
_____

Bible Verse: _____ **Today's Date:** _____

SAY, PRAY, & WRITE THE VERSE:

_____
_____
_____
_____
_____
_____
_____
_____
_____

Bible Verse: _____ Today's Date: _____

SAY, PRAY, & WRITE THE VERSE:

_____
_____
_____
_____
_____
_____
_____
_____
_____

Bible Verse: _____ Today's Date: _____

SAY, PRAY, & WRITE THE VERSE:

_____
_____
_____
_____
_____
_____
_____
_____
_____

Bible Verse: _____ Today's Date: _____

SAY, PRAY, & WRITE THE VERSE:

_____
_____
_____
_____
_____
_____
_____
_____
_____

Bible Verse: _____ **Today's Date:** _____

SAY, PRAY, & WRITE THE VERSE:

_____
_____
_____
_____
_____
_____
_____
_____
_____

Bible Verse: _____ **Today's Date:** _____

SAY, PRAY, & WRITE THE VERSE:

_____
_____
_____
_____
_____
_____
_____
_____
_____

Bible Verse: _____ **Today's Date:** _____

SAY, PRAY, & WRITE THE VERSE:

_____
_____
_____
_____
_____
_____
_____
_____
_____

Bible Verse: _____ **Today's Date:** _____

SAY, PRAY, & WRITE THE VERSE:

_____

_____

_____

_____

_____

_____

_____

_____

Bible Verse: _____ **Today's Date:** _____

SAY, PRAY, & WRITE THE VERSE:

_____

_____

_____

_____

_____

_____

_____

_____

Bible Verse: _____ **Today's Date:** _____

SAY, PRAY, & WRITE THE VERSE:

_____

_____

_____

_____

_____

_____

_____

_____

Bible Verse: _____ **Today's Date:** _____

SAY, PRAY, & WRITE THE VERSE:

_____

_____

_____

_____

_____

_____

_____

_____

Bible Verse: _____ **Today's Date:** _____

SAY, PRAY, & WRITE THE VERSE:

_____

_____

_____

_____

_____

_____

_____

_____

Bible Verse: _____ **Today's Date:** _____

SAY, PRAY, & WRITE THE VERSE:

_____

_____

_____

_____

_____

_____

_____

_____

Bible Verse: _____ **Today's Date:** _____

SAY, PRAY, & WRITE THE VERSE:

_____

_____

_____

_____

_____

_____

_____

Bible Verse: _____ **Today's Date:** _____

SAY, PRAY, & WRITE THE VERSE:

_____

_____

_____

_____

_____

_____

_____

Bible Verse: _____ **Today's Date:** _____

SAY, PRAY, & WRITE THE VERSE:

_____

_____

_____

_____

_____

_____

_____

Bible Verse: _____ **Today's Date:** _____

SAY, PRAY, & WRITE THE VERSE:

_____
_____
_____
_____
_____
_____
_____
_____
_____

Bible Verse: _____ **Today's Date:** _____

SAY, PRAY, & WRITE THE VERSE:

_____
_____
_____
_____
_____
_____
_____
_____
_____

Bible Verse: _____ **Today's Date:** _____

SAY, PRAY, & WRITE THE VERSE:

_____
_____
_____
_____
_____
_____
_____
_____
_____

Bible Verse: _____ Today's Date: _____

SAY, PRAY, & WRITE THE VERSE:

_____
_____
_____
_____
_____
_____
_____
_____
_____

Bible Verse: _____ Today's Date: _____

SAY, PRAY, & WRITE THE VERSE:

_____
_____
_____
_____
_____
_____
_____
_____
_____

Bible Verse: _____ Today's Date: _____

SAY, PRAY, & WRITE THE VERSE:

_____
_____
_____
_____
_____
_____
_____
_____
_____

Bible Verse: _____ **Today's Date:** _____

SAY, PRAY, & WRITE THE VERSE:

_____
_____
_____
_____
_____
_____
_____
_____

Bible Verse: _____ **Today's Date:** _____

SAY, PRAY, & WRITE THE VERSE:

_____
_____
_____
_____
_____
_____
_____
_____

Bible Verse: _____ **Today's Date:** _____

SAY, PRAY, & WRITE THE VERSE:

_____
_____
_____
_____
_____
_____
_____
_____

Bible Verse: _____ Today's Date: _____

SAY, PRAY, & WRITE THE VERSE:

_____
_____
_____
_____
_____
_____
_____
_____

Bible Verse: _____ Today's Date: _____

SAY, PRAY, & WRITE THE VERSE:

_____
_____
_____
_____
_____
_____
_____
_____

Bible Verse: _____ Today's Date: _____

SAY, PRAY, & WRITE THE VERSE:

_____
_____
_____
_____
_____
_____
_____
_____

Bible Verse: _____ **Today's Date:** _____

SAY, PRAY, & WRITE THE VERSE:

Bible Verse: _____ **Today's Date:** _____

SAY, PRAY, & WRITE THE VERSE:

Bible Verse: _____ **Today's Date:** _____

SAY, PRAY, & WRITE THE VERSE:

Bible Verse: _____ **Today's Date:** _____

SAY, PRAY, & WRITE THE VERSE:

_____

_____

_____

_____

_____

_____

_____

_____

Bible Verse: _____ **Today's Date:** _____

SAY, PRAY, & WRITE THE VERSE:

_____

_____

_____

_____

_____

_____

_____

_____

Bible Verse: _____ **Today's Date:** _____

SAY, PRAY, & WRITE THE VERSE:

_____

_____

_____

_____

_____

_____

_____

_____

Bible Verse: _____ **Today's Date:** _____

SAY, PRAY, & WRITE THE VERSE:

_____
_____
_____
_____
_____
_____
_____
_____
_____
_____

Bible Verse: _____ **Today's Date:** _____

SAY, PRAY, & WRITE THE VERSE:

_____
_____
_____
_____
_____
_____
_____
_____
_____
_____

Bible Verse: _____ **Today's Date:** _____

SAY, PRAY, & WRITE THE VERSE:

_____
_____
_____
_____
_____
_____
_____
_____
_____
_____

Bible Verse: _____ **Today's Date:** _____

SAY, PRAY, & WRITE THE VERSE:

Bible Verse: _____ **Today's Date:** _____

SAY, PRAY, & WRITE THE VERSE:

Bible Verse: _____ **Today's Date:** _____

SAY, PRAY, & WRITE THE VERSE:

Bible Verse: _____ **Today's Date:** _____

SAY, PRAY, & WRITE THE VERSE:

Bible Verse: _____ **Today's Date:** _____

SAY, PRAY, & WRITE THE VERSE:

Bible Verse: _____ **Today's Date:** _____

SAY, PRAY, & WRITE THE VERSE:

Bible Verse: _____ **Today's Date:** _____

SAY, PRAY, & WRITE THE VERSE:

_____

_____

_____

_____

_____

_____

_____

_____

Bible Verse: _____ **Today's Date:** _____

SAY, PRAY, & WRITE THE VERSE:

_____

_____

_____

_____

_____

_____

_____

_____

Bible Verse: _____ **Today's Date:** _____

SAY, PRAY, & WRITE THE VERSE:

_____

_____

_____

_____

_____

_____

_____

_____

Bible Verse: _____ **Today's Date:** _____

SAY, PRAY, & WRITE THE VERSE:

_____
_____
_____
_____
_____
_____
_____
_____
_____

Bible Verse: _____ **Today's Date:** _____

SAY, PRAY, & WRITE THE VERSE:

_____
_____
_____
_____
_____
_____
_____
_____
_____

Bible Verse: _____ **Today's Date:** _____

SAY, PRAY, & WRITE THE VERSE:

_____
_____
_____
_____
_____
_____
_____
_____
_____

Bible Verse: _____ **Today's Date:** _____

SAY, PRAY, & WRITE THE VERSE:

_____
_____
_____
_____
_____
_____
_____
_____

Bible Verse: _____ **Today's Date:** _____

SAY, PRAY, & WRITE THE VERSE:

_____
_____
_____
_____
_____
_____
_____
_____

Bible Verse: _____ **Today's Date:** _____

SAY, PRAY, & WRITE THE VERSE:

_____
_____
_____
_____
_____
_____
_____

Bible Verse: _____ **Today's Date:** _____

SAY, PRAY, & WRITE THE VERSE:

_____
_____
_____
_____
_____
_____
_____
_____
_____
_____

Bible Verse: _____ **Today's Date:** _____

SAY, PRAY, & WRITE THE VERSE:

_____
_____
_____
_____
_____
_____
_____
_____
_____
_____

Bible Verse: _____ **Today's Date:** _____

SAY, PRAY, & WRITE THE VERSE:

_____
_____
_____
_____
_____
_____
_____
_____
_____
_____

Bible Verse: _____ Today's Date: _____

SAY, PRAY, & WRITE THE VERSE:

_____
_____
_____
_____
_____
_____
_____
_____
_____

Bible Verse: _____ Today's Date: _____

SAY, PRAY, & WRITE THE VERSE:

_____
_____
_____
_____
_____
_____
_____
_____
_____

Bible Verse: _____ Today's Date: _____

SAY, PRAY, & WRITE THE VERSE:

_____
_____
_____
_____
_____
_____
_____
_____
_____

| Bible Verse: _____ Today's Date: _____ |

SAY, PRAY, & WRITE THE VERSE:

| Bible Verse: _____ Today's Date: _____ |

SAY, PRAY, & WRITE THE VERSE:

| Bible Verse: _____ Today's Date: _____ |

SAY, PRAY, & WRITE THE VERSE:

Bible Verse: _____ **Today's Date:** _____

SAY, PRAY, & WRITE THE VERSE:

_____

_____

_____

_____

_____

_____

_____

_____

Bible Verse: _____ **Today's Date:** _____

SAY, PRAY, & WRITE THE VERSE:

_____

_____

_____

_____

_____

_____

_____

_____

Bible Verse: _____ **Today's Date:** _____

SAY, PRAY, & WRITE THE VERSE:

_____

_____

_____

_____

_____

_____

_____

_____

Bible Verse: _____ **Today's Date:** _____

SAY, PRAY, & WRITE THE VERSE:

_____
_____
_____
_____
_____
_____
_____
_____
_____

Bible Verse: _____ **Today's Date:** _____

SAY, PRAY, & WRITE THE VERSE:

_____
_____
_____
_____
_____
_____
_____
_____
_____

Bible Verse: _____ **Today's Date:** _____

SAY, PRAY, & WRITE THE VERSE:

_____
_____
_____
_____
_____
_____
_____
_____
_____

Bible Verse: _____ **Today's Date:** _____

SAY, PRAY, & WRITE THE VERSE:

_____
_____
_____
_____
_____
_____
_____
_____
_____

Bible Verse: _____ **Today's Date:** _____

SAY, PRAY, & WRITE THE VERSE:

_____
_____
_____
_____
_____
_____
_____
_____
_____

Bible Verse: _____ **Today's Date:** _____

SAY, PRAY, & WRITE THE VERSE:

_____
_____
_____
_____
_____
_____
_____
_____
_____

Bible Verse: _____ **Today's Date:** _____

SAY, PRAY, & WRITE THE VERSE:

Bible Verse: _____ **Today's Date:** _____

SAY, PRAY, & WRITE THE VERSE:

Bible Verse: _____ **Today's Date:** _____

SAY, PRAY, & WRITE THE VERSE:

Bible Verse: _____ Today's Date: _____

SAY, PRAY, & WRITE THE VERSE:

_____
_____
_____
_____
_____
_____
_____
_____
_____
_____

Bible Verse: _____ Today's Date: _____

SAY, PRAY, & WRITE THE VERSE:

_____
_____
_____
_____
_____
_____
_____
_____
_____
_____

Bible Verse: _____ Today's Date: _____

SAY, PRAY, & WRITE THE VERSE:

_____
_____
_____
_____
_____
_____
_____
_____
_____

Bible Verse: _____ **Today's Date:** _____

SAY, PRAY, & WRITE THE VERSE:

_____
_____
_____
_____
_____
_____
_____
_____
_____

Bible Verse: _____ **Today's Date:** _____

SAY, PRAY, & WRITE THE VERSE:

_____
_____
_____
_____
_____
_____
_____
_____
_____

Bible Verse: _____ **Today's Date:** _____

SAY, PRAY, & WRITE THE VERSE:

_____
_____
_____
_____
_____
_____
_____
_____

Bible Verse: _____ **Today's Date:** _____

SAY, PRAY, & WRITE THE VERSE:

_____
_____
_____
_____
_____
_____
_____
_____
_____

Bible Verse: _____ **Today's Date:** _____

SAY, PRAY, & WRITE THE VERSE:

_____
_____
_____
_____
_____
_____
_____
_____
_____

Bible Verse: _____ **Today's Date:** _____

SAY, PRAY, & WRITE THE VERSE:

_____
_____
_____
_____
_____
_____
_____
_____
_____

Bible Verse: _____ **Today's Date:** _____

SAY, PRAY, & WRITE THE VERSE:

_____
_____
_____
_____
_____
_____
_____
_____
_____

Bible Verse: _____ **Today's Date:** _____

SAY, PRAY, & WRITE THE VERSE:

_____
_____
_____
_____
_____
_____
_____
_____
_____

Bible Verse: _____ **Today's Date:** _____

SAY, PRAY, & WRITE THE VERSE:

_____
_____
_____
_____
_____
_____
_____
_____
_____

Bible Verse: _____ **Today's Date:** _____

SAY, PRAY, & WRITE THE VERSE:

_____

_____

_____

_____

_____

_____

_____

_____

Bible Verse: _____ **Today's Date:** _____

SAY, PRAY, & WRITE THE VERSE:

_____

_____

_____

_____

_____

_____

_____

_____

Bible Verse: _____ **Today's Date:** _____

SAY, PRAY, & WRITE THE VERSE:

_____

_____

_____

_____

_____

_____

_____

_____

Bible Verse: _____ **Today's Date:** _____

SAY, PRAY, & WRITE THE VERSE:

_____
_____
_____
_____
_____
_____
_____
_____

Bible Verse: _____ **Today's Date:** _____

SAY, PRAY, & WRITE THE VERSE:

_____
_____
_____
_____
_____
_____
_____
_____

Bible Verse: _____ **Today's Date:** _____

SAY, PRAY, & WRITE THE VERSE:

_____
_____
_____
_____
_____
_____
_____
_____

Bible Verse: _____ **Today's Date:** _____

SAY, PRAY, & WRITE THE VERSE:

_____
_____
_____
_____
_____
_____
_____
_____
_____

Bible Verse: _____ **Today's Date:** _____

SAY, PRAY, & WRITE THE VERSE:

_____
_____
_____
_____
_____
_____
_____
_____
_____

Bible Verse: _____ **Today's Date:** _____

SAY, PRAY, & WRITE THE VERSE:

_____
_____
_____
_____
_____
_____
_____
_____
_____

Bible Verse: _____ **Today's Date:** _____

SAY, PRAY, & WRITE THE VERSE:

_____
_____
_____
_____
_____
_____
_____
_____
_____
_____

Bible Verse: _____ **Today's Date:** _____

SAY, PRAY, & WRITE THE VERSE:

_____
_____
_____
_____
_____
_____
_____
_____
_____
_____

Bible Verse: _____ **Today's Date:** _____

SAY, PRAY, & WRITE THE VERSE:

_____
_____
_____
_____
_____
_____
_____
_____
_____
_____

Bible Verse: _____ **Today's Date:** _____

SAY, PRAY, & WRITE THE VERSE:

_____
_____
_____
_____
_____
_____
_____
_____
_____

Bible Verse: _____ **Today's Date:** _____

SAY, PRAY, & WRITE THE VERSE:

_____
_____
_____
_____
_____
_____
_____
_____
_____

Bible Verse: _____ **Today's Date:** _____

SAY, PRAY, & WRITE THE VERSE:

_____
_____
_____
_____
_____
_____
_____
_____
_____

Bible Verse: _____ **Today's Date:** _____

SAY, PRAY, & WRITE THE VERSE:

_____
_____
_____
_____
_____
_____
_____
_____
_____

Bible Verse: _____ **Today's Date:** _____

SAY, PRAY, & WRITE THE VERSE:

_____
_____
_____
_____
_____
_____
_____
_____
_____

Bible Verse: _____ **Today's Date:** _____

SAY, PRAY, & WRITE THE VERSE:

_____
_____
_____
_____
_____
_____
_____
_____
_____

Bible Verse: _____ **Today's Date:** _____

SAY, PRAY, & WRITE THE VERSE:

_____

_____

_____

_____

_____

_____

_____

_____

Bible Verse: _____ **Today's Date:** _____

SAY, PRAY, & WRITE THE VERSE:

_____

_____

_____

_____

_____

_____

_____

_____

Bible Verse: _____ **Today's Date:** _____

SAY, PRAY, & WRITE THE VERSE:

_____

_____

_____

_____

_____

_____

_____

_____

Bible Verse: _____ **Today's Date:** _____

SAY, PRAY, & WRITE THE VERSE:

_____
_____
_____
_____
_____
_____
_____
_____
_____

Bible Verse: _____ **Today's Date:** _____

SAY, PRAY, & WRITE THE VERSE:

_____
_____
_____
_____
_____
_____
_____
_____
_____

Bible Verse: _____ **Today's Date:** _____

SAY, PRAY, & WRITE THE VERSE:

_____
_____
_____
_____
_____
_____
_____
_____
_____

Bible Verse: _____ Today's Date: _____

SAY, PRAY, & WRITE THE VERSE:

_____
_____
_____
_____
_____
_____
_____
_____
_____

Bible Verse: _____ Today's Date: _____

SAY, PRAY, & WRITE THE VERSE:

_____
_____
_____
_____
_____
_____
_____
_____
_____

Bible Verse: _____ Today's Date: _____

SAY, PRAY, & WRITE THE VERSE:

_____
_____
_____
_____
_____
_____
_____
_____
_____

Bible Verse: _____ **Today's Date:** _____

SAY, PRAY, & WRITE THE VERSE:

_____
_____
_____
_____
_____
_____
_____
_____

Bible Verse: _____ **Today's Date:** _____

SAY, PRAY, & WRITE THE VERSE:

_____
_____
_____
_____
_____
_____
_____
_____

Bible Verse: _____ **Today's Date:** _____

SAY, PRAY, & WRITE THE VERSE:

_____
_____
_____
_____
_____
_____
_____
_____

Bible Verse: _____ **Today's Date:** _____

SAY, PRAY, & WRITE THE VERSE:

_____

_____

_____

_____

_____

_____

_____

_____

Bible Verse: _____ **Today's Date:** _____

SAY, PRAY, & WRITE THE VERSE:

_____

_____

_____

_____

_____

_____

_____

_____

Bible Verse: _____ **Today's Date:** _____

SAY, PRAY, & WRITE THE VERSE:

_____

_____

_____

_____

_____

_____

_____

Bible Verse: _____ **Today's Date:** _____

SAY, PRAY, & WRITE THE VERSE:

_____
_____
_____
_____
_____
_____
_____
_____
_____

Bible Verse: _____ **Today's Date:** _____

SAY, PRAY, & WRITE THE VERSE:

_____
_____
_____
_____
_____
_____
_____
_____
_____

Bible Verse: _____ **Today's Date:** _____

SAY, PRAY, & WRITE THE VERSE:

_____
_____
_____
_____
_____
_____
_____
_____
_____

Bible Verse: _____ **Today's Date:** _____

SAY, PRAY, & WRITE THE VERSE:

_____
_____
_____
_____
_____
_____
_____
_____

Bible Verse: _____ **Today's Date:** _____

SAY, PRAY, & WRITE THE VERSE:

_____
_____
_____
_____
_____
_____
_____
_____

Bible Verse: _____ **Today's Date:** _____

SAY, PRAY, & WRITE THE VERSE:

_____
_____
_____
_____
_____
_____
_____
_____

Bible Verse: _____ **Today's Date:** _____

SAY, PRAY, & WRITE THE VERSE:

_____
_____
_____
_____
_____
_____
_____
_____
_____
_____

Bible Verse: _____ **Today's Date:** _____

SAY, PRAY, & WRITE THE VERSE:

_____
_____
_____
_____
_____
_____
_____
_____
_____
_____

Bible Verse: _____ **Today's Date:** _____

SAY, PRAY, & WRITE THE VERSE:

_____
_____
_____
_____
_____
_____
_____
_____
_____
_____

Bible Verse: _____ Today's Date: _____

SAY, PRAY, & WRITE THE VERSE:

_____
_____
_____
_____
_____
_____
_____
_____
_____

Bible Verse: _____ Today's Date: _____

SAY, PRAY, & WRITE THE VERSE:

_____
_____
_____
_____
_____
_____
_____
_____
_____

Bible Verse: _____ Today's Date: _____

SAY, PRAY, & WRITE THE VERSE:

_____
_____
_____
_____
_____
_____
_____
_____
_____

Bible Verse: _____ **Today's Date:** _____

SAY, PRAY, & WRITE THE VERSE:

_____
_____
_____
_____
_____
_____
_____
_____
_____

Bible Verse: _____ **Today's Date:** _____

SAY, PRAY, & WRITE THE VERSE:

_____
_____
_____
_____
_____
_____
_____
_____
_____

Bible Verse: _____ **Today's Date:** _____

SAY, PRAY, & WRITE THE VERSE:

_____
_____
_____
_____
_____
_____
_____
_____
_____

Bible Verse: _____ **Today's Date:** _____

SAY, PRAY, & WRITE THE VERSE:

_____
_____
_____
_____
_____
_____
_____
_____

Bible Verse: _____ **Today's Date:** _____

SAY, PRAY, & WRITE THE VERSE:

_____
_____
_____
_____
_____
_____
_____
_____

Bible Verse: _____ **Today's Date:** _____

SAY, PRAY, & WRITE THE VERSE:

_____
_____
_____
_____
_____
_____
_____

Bible Verse: _____ **Today's Date:** _____

SAY, PRAY, & WRITE THE VERSE:

Bible Verse: _____ **Today's Date:** _____

SAY, PRAY, & WRITE THE VERSE:

Bible Verse: _____ **Today's Date:** _____

SAY, PRAY, & WRITE THE VERSE:

Bible Verse: _____ **Today's Date:** _____

SAY, PRAY, & WRITE THE VERSE:

_____

_____

_____

_____

_____

_____

_____

_____

Bible Verse: _____ **Today's Date:** _____

SAY, PRAY, & WRITE THE VERSE:

_____

_____

_____

_____

_____

_____

_____

_____

Bible Verse: _____ **Today's Date:** _____

SAY, PRAY, & WRITE THE VERSE:

_____

_____

_____

_____

_____

_____

_____

Bible Verse: _____ **Today's Date:** _____

SAY, PRAY, & WRITE THE VERSE:

_____
_____
_____
_____
_____
_____
_____
_____
_____

Bible Verse: _____ **Today's Date:** _____

SAY, PRAY, & WRITE THE VERSE:

_____
_____
_____
_____
_____
_____
_____
_____
_____

Bible Verse: _____ **Today's Date:** _____

SAY, PRAY, & WRITE THE VERSE:

_____
_____
_____
_____
_____
_____
_____
_____
_____

Bible Verse: _____ **Today's Date:** _____

SAY, PRAY, & WRITE THE VERSE:

_____
_____
_____
_____
_____
_____
_____
_____
_____

Bible Verse: _____ **Today's Date:** _____

SAY, PRAY, & WRITE THE VERSE:

_____
_____
_____
_____
_____
_____
_____
_____
_____

Bible Verse: _____ **Today's Date:** _____

SAY, PRAY, & WRITE THE VERSE:

_____
_____
_____
_____
_____
_____
_____
_____

Bible Verse: _____ **Today's Date:** _____

SAY, PRAY, & WRITE THE VERSE:

_____
_____
_____
_____
_____
_____
_____
_____
_____

Bible Verse: _____ **Today's Date:** _____

SAY, PRAY, & WRITE THE VERSE:

_____
_____
_____
_____
_____
_____
_____
_____
_____

Bible Verse: _____ **Today's Date:** _____

SAY, PRAY, & WRITE THE VERSE:

_____
_____
_____
_____
_____
_____
_____
_____
_____

Bible Verse: _____ **Today's Date:** _____

SAY, PRAY, & WRITE THE VERSE:

_____
_____
_____
_____
_____
_____
_____
_____

Bible Verse: _____ **Today's Date:** _____

SAY, PRAY, & WRITE THE VERSE:

_____
_____
_____
_____
_____
_____
_____
_____

Bible Verse: _____ **Today's Date:** _____

SAY, PRAY, & WRITE THE VERSE:

_____
_____
_____
_____
_____
_____
_____
_____

Bible Verse: _____ **Today's Date:** _____

SAY, PRAY, & WRITE THE VERSE:

Bible Verse: _____ **Today's Date:** _____

SAY, PRAY, & WRITE THE VERSE:

Bible Verse: _____ **Today's Date:** _____

SAY, PRAY, & WRITE THE VERSE:

Bible Verse: _____ Today's Date: _____

SAY, PRAY, & WRITE THE VERSE:

_____
_____
_____
_____
_____
_____
_____
_____
_____
_____

Bible Verse: _____ Today's Date: _____

SAY, PRAY, & WRITE THE VERSE:

_____
_____
_____
_____
_____
_____
_____
_____
_____
_____

Bible Verse: _____ Today's Date: _____

SAY, PRAY, & WRITE THE VERSE:

_____
_____
_____
_____
_____
_____
_____
_____
_____

Bible Verse: _____ **Today's Date:** _____

SAY, PRAY, & WRITE THE VERSE:

Bible Verse: _____ **Today's Date:** _____

SAY, PRAY, & WRITE THE VERSE:

Bible Verse: _____ **Today's Date:** _____

SAY, PRAY, & WRITE THE VERSE:

Bible Verse: _____ **Today's Date:** _____

SAY, PRAY, & WRITE THE VERSE:

_____
_____
_____
_____
_____
_____
_____
_____
_____

Bible Verse: _____ **Today's Date:** _____

SAY, PRAY, & WRITE THE VERSE:

_____
_____
_____
_____
_____
_____
_____
_____
_____

Bible Verse: _____ **Today's Date:** _____

SAY, PRAY, & WRITE THE VERSE:

_____
_____
_____
_____
_____
_____
_____
_____
_____

Bible Verse: _____ Today's Date: _____

SAY, PRAY, & WRITE THE VERSE:

Bible Verse: _____ Today's Date: _____

SAY, PRAY, & WRITE THE VERSE:

Bible Verse: _____ Today's Date: _____

SAY, PRAY, & WRITE THE VERSE:

Bible Verse: _____ **Today's Date:** _____

SAY, PRAY, & WRITE THE VERSE:

Bible Verse: _____ **Today's Date:** _____

SAY, PRAY, & WRITE THE VERSE:

Bible Verse: _____ **Today's Date:** _____

SAY, PRAY, & WRITE THE VERSE:

Bible Verse: _____ **Today's Date:** _____

SAY, PRAY, & WRITE THE VERSE:

.
_____
_____
_____
_____
_____
_____
_____
_____

Bible Verse: _____ **Today's Date:** _____

SAY, PRAY, & WRITE THE VERSE:

_____
_____
_____
_____
_____
_____
_____
_____

Bible Verse: _____ **Today's Date:** _____

SAY, PRAY, & WRITE THE VERSE:

_____
_____
_____
_____
_____
_____
_____
_____

Bible Verse: _____ **Today's Date:** _____

SAY, PRAY, & WRITE THE VERSE:

_____
_____
_____
_____
_____
_____
_____
_____
_____

Bible Verse: _____ **Today's Date:** _____

SAY, PRAY, & WRITE THE VERSE:

_____
_____
_____
_____
_____
_____
_____
_____
_____

Bible Verse: _____ **Today's Date:** _____

SAY, PRAY, & WRITE THE VERSE:

_____
_____
_____
_____
_____
_____
_____
_____
_____

Bible Verse: _____ **Today's Date:** _____

SAY, PRAY, & WRITE THE VERSE:

Bible Verse: _____ **Today's Date:** _____

SAY, PRAY, & WRITE THE VERSE:

Bible Verse: _____ **Today's Date:** _____

SAY, PRAY, & WRITE THE VERSE:

Bible Verse: _____ **Today's Date:** _____

SAY, PRAY, & WRITE THE VERSE:

_____

_____

_____

_____

_____

_____

_____

_____

_____

Bible Verse: _____ **Today's Date:** _____

SAY, PRAY, & WRITE THE VERSE:

_____

_____

_____

_____

_____

_____

_____

_____

_____

Bible Verse: _____ **Today's Date:** _____

SAY, PRAY, & WRITE THE VERSE:

_____

_____

_____

_____

_____

_____

_____

_____

_____

Bible Verse: _____ Today's Date: _____

SAY, PRAY, & WRITE THE VERSE:

_____
_____
_____
_____
_____
_____
_____
_____
_____

Bible Verse: _____ Today's Date: _____

SAY, PRAY, & WRITE THE VERSE:

_____
_____
_____
_____
_____
_____
_____
_____
_____

Bible Verse: _____ Today's Date: _____

SAY, PRAY, & WRITE THE VERSE:

_____
_____
_____
_____
_____
_____
_____
_____

Bible Verse: _____ **Today's Date:** _____

SAY, PRAY, & WRITE THE VERSE:

_____

_____

_____

_____

_____

_____

_____

_____

Bible Verse: _____ **Today's Date:** _____

SAY, PRAY, & WRITE THE VERSE:

_____

_____

_____

_____

_____

_____

_____

_____

Bible Verse: _____ **Today's Date:** _____

SAY, PRAY, & WRITE THE VERSE:

_____

_____

_____

_____

_____

_____

_____

_____

Bible Verse: _____ **Today's Date:** _____

SAY, PRAY, & WRITE THE VERSE:

Bible Verse: _____ **Today's Date:** _____

SAY, PRAY, & WRITE THE VERSE:

Bible Verse: _____ **Today's Date:** _____

SAY, PRAY, & WRITE THE VERSE:

Bible Verse: _____ Today's Date: _____

SAY, PRAY, & WRITE THE VERSE:

_____
_____
_____
_____
_____
_____
_____
_____
_____

Bible Verse: _____ Today's Date: _____

SAY, PRAY, & WRITE THE VERSE:

_____
_____
_____
_____
_____
_____
_____
_____
_____

Bible Verse: _____ Today's Date: _____

SAY, PRAY, & WRITE THE VERSE:

_____
_____
_____
_____
_____
_____
_____
_____
_____

Bible Verse: _____ **Today's Date:** _____

SAY, PRAY, & WRITE THE VERSE:

_____
_____
_____
_____
_____
_____
_____
_____
_____

Bible Verse: _____ **Today's Date:** _____

SAY, PRAY, & WRITE THE VERSE:

_____
_____
_____
_____
_____
_____
_____
_____
_____

Bible Verse: _____ **Today's Date:** _____

SAY, PRAY, & WRITE THE VERSE:

_____
_____
_____
_____
_____
_____
_____
_____
_____

Bible Verse: _____ Today's Date: _____

SAY, PRAY, & WRITE THE VERSE:

Bible Verse: _____ Today's Date: _____

SAY, PRAY, & WRITE THE VERSE:

Bible Verse: _____ Today's Date: _____

SAY, PRAY, & WRITE THE VERSE:

Bible Verse: _____ **Today's Date:** _____

SAY, PRAY, & WRITE THE VERSE:

Bible Verse: _____ **Today's Date:** _____

SAY, PRAY, & WRITE THE VERSE:

Bible Verse: _____ **Today's Date:** _____

SAY, PRAY, & WRITE THE VERSE:

Bible Verse: _____ **Today's Date:** _____

SAY, PRAY, & WRITE THE VERSE:

_____

_____

_____

_____

_____

_____

_____

_____

Bible Verse: _____ **Today's Date:** _____

SAY, PRAY, & WRITE THE VERSE:

_____

_____

_____

_____

_____

_____

_____

_____

Bible Verse: _____ **Today's Date:** _____

SAY, PRAY, & WRITE THE VERSE:

_____

_____

_____

_____

_____

_____

_____

_____

Bible Verse: _____ **Today's Date:** _____

SAY, PRAY, & WRITE THE VERSE:

_____
_____
_____
_____
_____
_____
_____
_____
_____
_____

Bible Verse: _____ **Today's Date:** _____

SAY, PRAY, & WRITE THE VERSE:

_____
_____
_____
_____
_____
_____
_____
_____
_____
_____

Bible Verse: _____ **Today's Date:** _____

SAY, PRAY, & WRITE THE VERSE:

_____
_____
_____
_____
_____
_____
_____
_____
_____
_____

Bible Verse: _____ **Today's Date:** _____

SAY, PRAY, & WRITE THE VERSE:

_____
_____
_____
_____
_____
_____
_____
_____
_____

Bible Verse: _____ **Today's Date:** _____

SAY, PRAY, & WRITE THE VERSE:

_____
_____
_____
_____
_____
_____
_____
_____
_____

Bible Verse: _____ **Today's Date:** _____

SAY, PRAY, & WRITE THE VERSE:

_____
_____
_____
_____
_____
_____
_____
_____
_____

Bible Verse: _____ **Today's Date:** _____

SAY, PRAY, & WRITE THE VERSE:

Bible Verse: _____ **Today's Date:** _____

SAY, PRAY, & WRITE THE VERSE:

Bible Verse: _____ **Today's Date:** _____

SAY, PRAY, & WRITE THE VERSE:

Bible Verse: _____ Today's Date: _____

SAY, PRAY, & WRITE THE VERSE:

Bible Verse: _____ Today's Date: _____

SAY, PRAY, & WRITE THE VERSE:

Bible Verse: _____ Today's Date: _____

SAY, PRAY, & WRITE THE VERSE:

Bible Verse: _____ **Today's Date:** _____

SAY, PRAY, & WRITE THE VERSE:

_____

_____

_____

_____

_____

_____

_____

_____

Bible Verse: _____ **Today's Date:** _____

SAY, PRAY, & WRITE THE VERSE:

_____

_____

_____

_____

_____

_____

_____

_____

Bible Verse: _____ **Today's Date:** _____

SAY, PRAY, & WRITE THE VERSE:

_____

_____

_____

_____

_____

_____

_____

_____

Bible Verse: _____ **Today's Date:** _____

SAY, PRAY, & WRITE THE VERSE:

Bible Verse: _____ **Today's Date:** _____

SAY, PRAY, & WRITE THE VERSE:

Bible Verse: _____ **Today's Date:** _____

SAY, PRAY, & WRITE THE VERSE:

Bible Verse: _____ **Today's Date:** _____

SAY, PRAY, & WRITE THE VERSE:

Bible Verse: _____ **Today's Date:** _____

SAY, PRAY, & WRITE THE VERSE

Bible Verse: _____ **Today's Date:** _____

SAY, PRAY, & WRITE THE VERSE:

Bible Verse: _____ Today's Date: _____

SAY, PRAY, & WRITE THE VERSE:

_____
_____
_____
_____
_____
_____
_____
_____
_____
_____

Bible Verse: _____ Today's Date: _____

SAY, PRAY, & WRITE THE VERSE:

_____
_____
_____
_____
_____
_____
_____
_____
_____
_____

Bible Verse: _____ Today's Date: _____

SAY, PRAY, & WRITE THE VERSE:

_____
_____
_____
_____
_____
_____
_____
_____
_____
_____

Bible Verse: _____ Today's Date: _____

SAY, PRAY, & WRITE THE VERSE:

Bible Verse: _____ Today's Date: _____

SAY, PRAY, & WRITE THE VERSE:

Bible Verse: _____ Today's Date: _____

SAY, PRAY, & WRITE THE VERSE:

Bible Verse: _____ **Today's Date:** _____

SAY, PRAY, & WRITE THE VERSE:

_____

_____

_____

_____

_____

_____

_____

_____

Bible Verse: _____ **Today's Date:** _____

SAY, PRAY, & WRITE THE VERSE:

_____

_____

_____

_____

_____

_____

_____

_____

Bible Verse: _____ **Today's Date:** _____

SAY, PRAY, & WRITE THE VERSE:

_____

_____

_____

_____

_____

_____

_____

_____

Bible Verse: _____ **Today's Date:** _____

SAY, PRAY, & WRITE THE VERSE:

_____
_____
_____
_____
_____
_____
_____
_____

Bible Verse: _____ **Today's Date:** _____

SAY, PRAY, & WRITE THE VERSE:

_____
_____
_____
_____
_____
_____
_____
_____

Bible Verse: _____ **Today's Date:** _____

SAY, PRAY, & WRITE THE VERSE:

_____
_____
_____
_____
_____
_____
_____
_____

Made in the USA
Las Vegas, NV
08 January 2023

65177415R00073